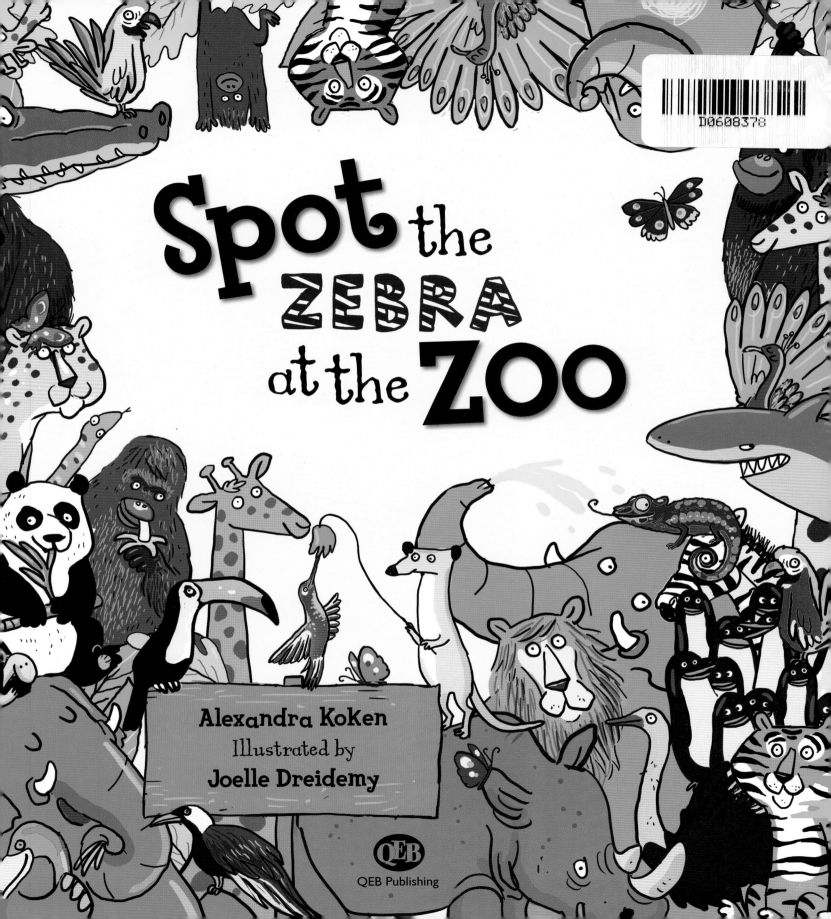

Spot the ZEBRA at the ZOO

Alexandra Koken

Illustrated by

Joelle Dreidemy

QEB
QEB Publishing

African Animals

Big Cats

Birds

This zebra is hiding inside the book. Can you find him in every scene?

Elephants can swim underwater, with only their trunks above the surface.

Can you spot these things? butterfly bird brush apple bow

DAILY PENGUIN

Penguins sometimes slide on their tummies! This is called tobogganing.

Can you spot these things?

fish   bucket   clock   boat   flower

Lions are the only big cats that live in groups.

Can you spot these things?

- pink shell
- red and white fish
- sea horse
- sea sponge
- orange eel

How many jellyfish are there?

A shark can grow thousands of teeth in its life.

Young flamingos have gray feathers.

Can you spot these things?

pink flower

mouse

cup

yarn

glass jar

car

Pythons eat huge meals. They can swallow a whole pig!

Can you spot these things?
sunblock
orange flag
teapot
teddy bear
pitcher
Wildebeest travel across Africa every year in search of food.
A giraffe's tongue is dark blue and 20 inches long. That's as long as a grown-up's arm!

Butterflies taste with their feet, not their tongues!

Gorillas sleep in nests high up in the trees.

More to Spot

Go back and find these scenes in the book!

Did you find me?

More Zoo Fun!

Animal Talk

Some of the animals in this book ask you a question. If animals could talk in real life, what would they say? Try dressing up as an animal and talking like one!

Hide-and-Seek

Choose a stuffed animal that you can hide around your home for a friend or family member to spot, just like the zebra in the book! You could hide other objects and make a list of things to find.

Memory Game

Cut out 12 matching pieces of cardboard or paper. Make pairs by drawing the same zoo animal on two cards. Then lay the cards face-down on a table and mix them up. Find the pairs by turning over two cards at a time until you have matched them all.

Build Your Own Zoo

Make a zoo in your home! Use stuffed animals placed in different parts of your room, small plastic animals on a hand-drawn map, or draw the whole zoo. Think about where you want each animal to live. What kind of animals would you like in your zoo?

Designer: Krina Patel
Managing Editor: Victoria Garrard
Design Manager: Anna Lubecka

Copyright © QEB Publishing, Inc. 2013

First published in the United States by QEB Publishing, Inc.
3 Wrigley, Suite A
Irvine, CA 92618

www.qed-publishing.co.uk

A CIP record for this book is available from the Library of Congress.

ISBN 978 1 60992 636 6

Printed in China